"… so tell us something
about yourself…"

"… so tell us something about yourself…"

Aparna Muralidhar

PARTRIDGE

A Penguin Random House Company

To order additional copies of this book, contact
Partridge India
000 800 10062 62
orders.india@partridgepublishing.com

www.partridgepublishing.com/india

Contents

The Buffalo Soldier law 1

The hills are alive...(and so am I) 5

"Where's the patient, Ma'am?" 11

"...so tell us something about yourself..." 17

R.I.P. privacy... 21

I Pinched a Mannequin.. 25

Keep Walking - one for the road 31

A brief history of some things Bill Bryson left out 35

"Falls alarms, do not picnic".. 43

The Tragedy of the Commons.. 47

Vote for Tony Blair.. 51

Insomniacs, Killjoys, and other friendly people 57

For Mozart, press 5 63

I Have a Dream.. 69

Laughter, the bitter medicine... 75

The Salesman 79

10 things you must know if you're a road user
    in Bengaluru... 85

The Psychometry.. 89

Breaking News... 93

Who Are You?.. 97

"There's a Bomb on the Bus.....".................................... 101

The Humble Monkey Stands Up To Be Counted........ 107

A Wedding and Other Hair-Raising Events in
    God's Own Country.. 111

The Buffalo Soldier law

In a move that has created a controversy of epic proportions, the Indian government today changed the national animal from tiger to buffalo through a backdoor ordinance that was not sent to the houses for a vote. Dubbed the "Buffalo Soldier" law, the ordinance takes immediate effect. Utter chaos prevailed on the streets of every major city and town as the bewildered new national animals were paraded by their owners in celebratory processions. Stampedes were reported from at least 13 places in which 10 buffaloes and twice the number of people have lost their lives. The topic is trending on Twitter.

It all began when 7 buffaloes belonging to a minister staged a walkout from the minister's well guarded farm. They were protesting the maltreatment of human beings in the minister's hometown. The buffaloes belong to a group called AETP (Animals for the Ethical Treatment of People). The animals were traced and brought back after a massive manhunt by PETA (People for the Ethical Treatment of Animals). The grateful minister has sworn to ban AETP as a "rogue outlaw oufit." It is reliably learnt that the AETP

1

responded to the news by releasing unprecedented amounts of methane into the atmosphere. In the national capital, the Chief Minister's brooms are finally being put to use. When asked whether the AETP could not be enlisted to help trace dozens of missing children in his hometown, the minister dead-panned, "What children?"

Meanwhile, a relatively unknown tiger group called ISH (I'm Still Here) has petitioned the President against the "grave injustice and racial discrimination" and has threatened to take to the streets to have the ordinance reversed. Tiger activists are reportedly excited and hope to finally stop fudging their figures as the opportunity presents itself for a transparent census. When asked to comment, the Prime Minister was typically sagacious, "In a democracy, all voices must be heard," he intoned. "Be thankful we haven't gone to the dogs," he added demurely.

In early 2014, seven buffaloes that belonged to a minister in India's largest state, Uttar Pradesh, were stolen. Several police teams were formed to conduct night-long searches for the missing buffaloes. Several dairies, slaughter houses and meat factories were raided. Three policemen on night patrol at the time of the incident were suspended. In the same state, hundreds of children have gone missing over the years. Many remain untraced to this day.

The hills are alive...(and so am I)

After driving through some of the most spectacular hairpin bends in the Western Ghats (nine in all), we realized our resort in Waynad, didn't want to be found. It was buried almost 10 km in the deep forests hundreds of meters up in the mountains. We overshot it the first time around because there's no board to announce it as you're coming in. We kept driving because the driver belonged to the male of the species and it was a blow to his ego to ask someone if we were lost though I kept gently (by my definition) suggesting to him that it did look like we were lost. By the time he made up his mind to swallow his pride and pop the question, we had driven to what seemed like the ends of the earth. When he stopped finally and asked "Which way to Kannampatta?" the guy answered with a question: "Kannampattay-yo? Why have you come HERE?" Believe me, that's the last thing you want to hear. If we knew the answer to that question, we wouldn't ask him. Then he said, "It's all the way back there." A sweeping wave of his hand suggested it could be anywhere in Asia (or Africa).

"Do we have to turn back?" I asked the driver and it took every ounce of effort not to say "I told you so."

"Just for a bit," he muttered under his breath and I'm sure it took every ounce of his effort not to say "Now, shut up and sit back till I get you seriously lost again." He drove for what seemed to be forever before he spotted the board announcing the resort had been found – I've never seen a happier man. But that's because he didn't know what lay in store. Unknown to the unsuspecting driver, it would be another 10 km after it was found that the resort would actually be found.

We entered the forests through a road that seemed two fingerbreadths wide – it was the narrowest path I've ever seen. It looked like it could accommodate nothing more than one horse. Thick woods, mud hills, rocks on one side and sheer drops on the other. This was the only entrance into the resort and - like we found out to our horror, later – the only exit as well. We were driving on what might as well have been a rope and hoping an ant wouldn't approach. If a walker came from the other side, we had four choices: a) He could climb over our car and keep walking. b) We could reverse 5 km with him riding on our hood or roof, to deposit him outside the trail. c) He could walk backwards 5 km because there wasn't enough space for him to turn around. d) Or we could do the easiest thing: run over him – in which case he would literally and metaphorically pass over to the other side. If a car came from the other side, we had one choice: head butt it off the cliff. I made a mental note to tell the resort that they must ferry their guests either on mules or horses, but if the horse were to meet a fellow horse coming from the opposite direction, we were done for; one of them would have to jump over the other or walk backwards all the way. I finally understood why Tarzan was a happy man.

The driver sighed and giggled alternately and sometimes emitted a sound between a sigh and a giggle that meant "I'd love to simply stop the car right here, get down, and run away, you nut jobs." And then it happened. To our collective horror, there was a car headed straight for us, from the opposite direction – apparently leaving the resort. "This is a new car. This is my first trip in the new car," the driver whimpered. It was directed at God. Then he turned to us. "This is a new car," he told us. "Congratulations!" I said brightly and sensed immediately it was the worst possible thing to say. I couldn't read his face. Let's just say he wasn't happy. (Let's also say if looks could kill, you would be reading my obituary now instead).

When the other car got close enough, our driver put his head out and yelled, "This is a new car!"

"Oh," the other fellow said, his face registering impending doom, "can you go closer on your side?"

"Can I? Yes, I can if I can drive up the mountains vertically, otherwise I can't," our driver snapped testily. "This is a new car" he said to no one in particular.

"Well, the only way I can go any closer on MY side is if I plunged off the mountain," the other driver murmured thoughtfully. We waited with bated breath but he changed his mind.

Then began the finest demonstration of negotiations I've ever witnessed - these guys ought to be our diplomats in Pakistan, they'd do a fantastic job. With great politeness, they directed each other where to turn, how to reverse, what to avoid and after what can only be described as 15 minutes of death dance, two cars miraculously passed on the bicycle track. I'm sure the road must've expanded – there's **no way** the cars would've passed otherwise.

By now, our driver was perspiring freely in the chilly hillside forest. But he was a happy man. At least for a while. After we'd gone about 300 meters, out of nowhere a calf darted out. It saw the car and began prancing around trying to climb up the steep slope, sliding back, hopping around (I think on two legs) and generally acting cute and confused. "This is a new car," our driver told the prancing calf and turned off the engine and leaned on the horn. The sound drove the calf crazy and it began darting about wildly like its tail was on fire.

"Don't jump on my car," the driver begged the calf. "This is a new car."

"He will if you keep up with the honking," I told him cheerfully and he quickly got off the God awful sound. And just like that, out of thin air, a man materialized with a lasso and began chasing the calf. It was a wild goose chase for the longest time as the man crouched, lunged, and sprinted trying to lasso the calf which kept bleating like a lamb as it ducked and dodged him expertly. After a while everyone forgot who was chasing whom. I think the calf forgot too and that's how he got caught. The man folded himself and the calf and they stuffed themselves into the woods so we could pass and so it came to pass that nature, man, beast, a new car and a harassed driver delivered us into the lovely mountains of Waynad.

"Where's the patient, Ma'am?"

PART I - ADMISSION

"Where's the patient, Ma'am?" the girl behind the desk asked me politely.

"I'm the patient, Ma'am," I smiled.

"Oh… are you alone?" she asked looking around.

"Not if you count the other 10,542 patients you're housing right now in your hospital," I said smiling.

"But why have you come alone? Why didn't you bring someone with you?"

"Because I'm the only one I know who needs hospitalization at this point in time."

"Oh…" she said again uncertainly, "so you're admitting yourself?"

"Surprise, surprise…" I said cheerfully giving her my best grin.

"Are you ill?" She looked worried, like I could be dangerously ill and she wouldn't know.

"No," I said, "just blind… in this eye" I pointed to my right eye.

"Oh!" her hand flew to her mouth and her eyes widened

in terror - like I had told her SHE was blind. "Why didn't you tell me, Ma'am?" she asked.

"I told you just now."

"Why didn't you tell me before?"

"Because you didn't ask me before."

"Madam," she said somewhat irritated at the witless exchange "I don't go around asking people 'Are you the patient and are you blind?'"

"Madam," I said "I don't go around telling people "I'm Aparna and I'm blind."

PART II - INPATIENT

"Where's the patient, Ma'am?" asked the nurse politely as she wheeled in the IV.

I pointed to myself, smiled and waved.

"Oh! Why are you walking around? Can you lie down? Why have you not changed into the hospital gown? Where is your attender?"

"Which question should I answer first?" I asked her.

"Madam, please change your clothes and lie down, I have to start the IV. Please tell your attender to come in. Doctor will come in now and he will want to speak with your attender."

"I'm the attender," I said.

She looked at me like I'd said I'm Mickey Mouse. "You said just now you're the patient," she said accusingly.

"I'm the patient and the attender," I said "Are we good now?"

"Who is with you?" she asked me and she was unnecessarily loud.

"You" I said very softly.

She gave me the I-want-to-hit-you-now look. "Where is your husband?" she demanded and I thanked my stars I didn't have one.

"I don't have one," I said.

"You're not married?" she asked incredulously "But your chart says you're 41!"

"How time flies," I said cheerfully.

PART III - MRI

"Sit in the wheelchair Ma'am, we're taking you to MRI," the bored wheelchair pusher yawned.

"I can walk, I don't need a wheelchair," I said and began walking.

"Sit in the wheelchair!!!" he said firmly, "you can't walk into the MRI room."

"Why not?" I asked perplexed.

He fixed me with a steely glare "Because you might not be able to walk back, you might be unsteady when you come out of the MRI machine."

"In that case, why don't YOU sit in the wheelchair and I'll push. We can swap on the return ride," I said smiling.

"Sister!!" he called "patient is refusing to sit in the wheelchair, sister," he whined.

"Patient is refusing to sit in the wheelchair sister," I mimicked in a soft sing-song under my breath and sat.

"Why would I be unsteady? We're not going on the Ferris wheel, are we? I know what an MRI is, okay?" I grumbled as he wheeled me whistling softly.

PART IV - POST-DISCHARGE

"Where's the patient, Ma'am?"

"I'm the patient, Ma'am" I was at the hospital pharmacy buying supplies for my infusion.

"Oh... so this IV is for you?"

"Bingo!"

"Do you know the infusion will take 4 hours? Why have you come alone?"

"Yes, I know the infusion will take 4 hours and that's exactly why I've come alone."

She looked a little miffed "We encourage patients to bring somebody with them; if something happens, we won't be responsible."

"Believe me, if something happens, you will be responsible and I will sue you," I said smiling.

MORAL OF STORY: Always wear a T-shirt that says "I'm the patient".... when you're going on the Ferris wheel.

"...so tell us something about yourself..."

Every mediocre job interview eventually comes around to: "....okay, so tell us something about yourself..."

I'd give my right arm to be able to say to them:

1. Oh, I'm an axe-murderer just out from a medically induced coma (very softly with a smile)

2. I'm a nun, a none, a none-nun.... hehehehehe... that's N-O-N-E space N-U-N... of your business.... hehehehe.... whatever

3. I'm... uh... I'm.... I'm sorry, what did I say my name was? (in wide-eyed panic)

4. I'm bored (yawning noisily)

5. I'm the Alpha and the Omega, I'm the Now and the Evermore, I'm Sin and Divinity, the All and the Nothing, the up and the down, the left and the right... err... should I go on? Or should I get down?

6. I'm hungry (jumping up and rummaging through drawers)

7. I'm your future boss. Say hello to me nicely (offering a handshake)

8. Ok. That's it! You'll hear from my lawyer (over my shoulder as I storm out)

9. I'm unarmed and dangerous... hehehehe.... just kidding.... hehehehe... I'm actually armed... hehehehe

10. I'm what somebody lost and you found.... I'm serendipity (batting my eyelids)

R.I.P. privacy

It's official - thanks to TIME - the legacy of decade 2000 is the reinvention of communication. Around the globe, people are "collecting" people, and how! You'd think homo sapiens is now an endangered species. In chatrooms, on cell phones and Blackberrys, on mailing lists and networking sites, people are talking to anyone who cares to listen, like never before. Celebrities are leading the yakking brigade. A plush sofa and a dolled-up talk show host are invitation enough for people to spill their guts on national and international television (the tissue industry has never had it so good).

India was rated the most garrulous nation in a recent poll. From decades of state-sponsored thought control to no-thought no-control, we've come a long way, baby. There are now 10,000 ways to connect to your neighbour who you can reach across and tap on the shoulder, but that's passe. Cell phones have unrecognizably altered the way people interact with one another. Privacy is now a bathroom break. It's perfectly acceptable for 6 people to sit at a table constantly texting or talking on their phones - to everyone except the people they're sitting with. It raises decibel levels but not eyebrows. You cannot sit in a restaurant or a theater or even stroll down a street without overhearing some unwanted detail of a stranger's life. Run but you can't hide. (I even get calls from songs).

YouTube - where you can get your 15 minutes of fame in less than 15 seconds - is our passport to global citizenship. Simply monkeying around with a handycam will guarantee you eyeballs, a fan club, and instant stardom. If that's not enough, you can minute your life in hair-splitting detail (and atrocious spelling) on the worldwide web - and then supplement it with pictures. Because it's insanely easy to be seen and heard, nothing needs to be left unsaid or unseen anymore. And as Voltaire said, anything too stupid to be said, can be sung. And taped. And broadcast. Live! Bling is king. Silly season is here to stay. Everyone's invited.

TIME magazine declared Mark Zuckerberg, CEO of Facebook, its Person of the Year for 2010 in a tribute to his invention that redefined the term "social networking" and grew to dizzying heights of success.

I Pinched a Mannequin

This is a DIY manual on how to ruin a perfect Sunday evening.

1. Sneak up to your comatose spouse and announce in your best "bright idea" voice... "LET'S GO SHHOPPPIIINNNGGG!!!!"

2. Pick a mall that you're sure the world and its mother will be at.

3. Wailing ambulance behind you.

4. Slow down and pull over to let it pass.

5. Wonder why he's chasing you and not passing you.

6. Check rearview mirror. No ambulance. Your sleeping angel has woken up in the backseat.

7. Yell at spouse.

8. Get yelled back at.

9. Drive into mall parking lot and join 2658 cars in front of you.

10. Pick a store in the mall that's offering 50% off on everything from pin to plane to lost babies whose parents forgot to pick them up after last week's shopping.

11. Pick your weapon of mass destruction - your shopping cart.

12. Go berserk filling it. Look for sales people to assist you.

13. Excitedly share with spouse your discovery of anti-male/female pattern balding lotion.

14. ....while spouse quietly hemorrhages visualizing hair growing everywhere except on your head.

15. Lean over and breathe into spouse's ear: "It's okay, honey. I'll still love you when you look like a bear."

16. Notice you can't tell difference between mannequins and sales people.

17. Sneak up to a figure and cough suddenly; figure doesn't flinch. Phew! Mannequin.

18. Sidle up to another mannequin and pinch it. Shoot! Mannequin jumps and yelps - NOT mannequin.

19. Apologise and ask where the cereal section is.

20. Apologise again - NOT mannequin, NOT sales person.

21. Resume hunt for sales person.

22. Spot zombie with badge and approach.

23. Scratch head as zombie refuses to open mouth and points vaguely in a northwesterly direction.

24. Head for billing.

25. Pick line where guy in front of you has billed 10,000 bucks...

26. ....and is paying for it in coupons...

27. .....in denominations of 10s and 20s...

28. ....and he's reached 6000 and lost count and has started over....

29. .....for the 5th time.

30. Oh Shoot! Where's your baby?

31. Panic.

32. Tear around the store like your neighbour's Rottweiler is on your tail.

33. Pray you've lost your spouse as well.

34. Crash into shopping carts and body parts.

35. Find wailing baby in "50% off on Cereals!" section...

36. ....barcoded and price tagged.

37. Grab baby and head back to billing...

38. .....that now has 1629 people in front of you.

If you're a man, you get off here. Congratulations! Your Sunday is now well and truly ruined. But what the hell... pop a beer can and tune into ESPN. WWF will seem like a picnic compared to what you've been through.

39. If you're a woman, read on. There's a lot of evening left to be ruined yet, so bring it on, baby!

40. Slam things around in your kitchen.

41. Yell at your maid.

42. Threaten your baby.

43. Burn the dinner.

44. If your spouse asks you what's wrong, say "nothing" and make it sound like a swear word.

Congratulations! Now, your Sunday and your spouse's Sunday, Monday, Tuesday and Wednesday are ruined!

And he hasn't even seen your shopping bill yet!

Keep Walking - one for the road

A lot of people I know have an amazing road sense. Me, I was born without an internal GPS. If you stand me in a spot, blindfold me, and spin me around a couple of times, I won't know which way to turn (I'll probably stagger around drunkenly for a few seconds, puke all over myself, and faint). People like me depend heavily on signage, landmarks, and auto drivers to get us to where we're going without crossing into the next state. But, it's not just my road sense, I'm hopeless at finding anything at all (which is why I'm not married); I couldn't spot a dancing moose in a discotheque because I wouldn't find the discotheque to begin with - even if one of those colored disco balls fell on my head.

One-way streets is a good concept but it can be terrifying for someone who has a great propensity to get lost because if you take the wrong road, there's literally no turning back and instead of going where you need to go, you'll end up going where the road takes you. (I'm better than my mom though - she once drove around a circle thrice before she realized she was going round and round.)

So if I have to go to a place which I haven't been to before, I usually do a recce the previous day. Problem is, it seems like I've never been to any place before - even the ones I've been to before. Which is how I set out to establish where the Government Arts and Science College is. I found the college but I didn't know I'd found it because it didn't have a board that said it was the Government Arts and Science College and it had been found; of course, all you had to do was to look at it to know it was a college but I need more proof - I need a board that proclaims what it is before you'll convince me and to my bad luck there was no board. And worse, now I had to find my way back home through the maze of one-ways. I simply kept following the road for 15 minutes without knowing where I was going.

I finally gave up and pulled up next to an auto driver and asked him "which way to Domlur?"

He looked at me like I'd asked him "Which way to Africa?" Then he giggled and pointed down the road and said, "Follow that road till you come to a U-turn, take the U-turn and go back to where you came from."

Very helpful.

"But where did I come from?" I asked him.

I think he wanted to say "I hope you don't want me to answer that," but he changed his mind and shrugged as if to say "anywhere you want it to be."

"... so tell us something about yourself..."

I peered at boards (the signage has really improved in the city) from which all kinds of names flew at me, some familiar ("so THAT's the railway station!") but mostly not. To cut a long story short, I followed the familiar sounding names and landed up in front of my aunt's house which is a good 10 km from home but it was still home - it was lunchtime by now, I was hungry and tired and happy.

Life's like that - you suddenly realize you're on the wrong road but whaddya know, it's a one-way street, so you keep going, and you stumble around following familiar sign boards guided by an inner intuition only to rediscover your faith in serendipity.

A brief history of some things Bill Bryson left out

Autorickshaw - a 3-wheeler public transport buggy; 'autos' are the only motorized vehicles that can simulate a horse ride without a saddle in the Andes on a horse that's trying to get away from gun fire. Alien to human emotions, 90-degree angles, and the rule book, auto drivers perch at angles ranging from 45 to 65 degrees to give their carefully folded passengers a lively and unforgettable ride through urban India's it's-all-happening-here streets.

Bollywood - A 5000-year-old Sanskrit term from India's rich cultural heritage that means 'dance,' Bollywood is the name of the biggest movie-making industry in the world – the Hindi movie industry. It is also the only movie industry in the world where 5782 directors have used the same script to make 10,865 films with 50,847 songs, 50,847 dances in 3498 locations with 85,432 costumes. This script was written in 362 B.C. by a man who wore bearskin, had long straggly hair, and regularly clubbed women to death.

Cell phones - mobile devices with which you can take pictures, listen to music, record events, send messages, play games, check your email, calculate sums, and watch a cricket match (if you're still interested). You can also make calls.

China - an Asian country that's so big, it's everybody's neighbour and nobody's friend. Having gotten a foot in the door of the world's economy, the Chinese are now in the active process of breaking down the door. From closet capitalists to closet socialists to plain in your closet, 'Made in China' is now a somebody-stop-me label on a 'the world is not enough' tour.

Cuba - a Caribbean Jerry that is a perpetual thorn in Uncle Tom's flesh. America's 5-decade embargo on Cuba makes U.S. trade with the island illegal. America's stated objective for the embargo is to bring (surprise, surprise) democracy to Cuba which (surprise, surprise, surprise) it has failed to do. After large oil reserves were found in North Cuba, Tom suddenly wants to be Jerry's friend.

Global warming - this new-age terrorist dumps ice and snow in deserts, dunks England's head in the swimming pool, unleashes winds that can transport Japan to China, and excites stock markets all over the world; has redefined "weapons of mass destruction" but has been unable to rearrange the molecules that make up George Bush.

Iran - a spunky little country where the star-spangled banner is the chief combustible material. It also produces oil and can toss a bomb quite far. When Iran kidnapped and released 15 British Navy personnel from custody for reasons unknown (of custody, not release), oil prices nose-dived indicating its power and clout in the world economy.

Japan - a work in progress quite literally with a population of extremely hard working people who never leave their assembly lines even when the earth shakes them up which it does every 5 minutes; they just smile, bow, and slow down. Tokyo, the capital of Japan, is the world's costliest city and is built to survive any sort of earthquake - there's no place for people or buildings to fall.

Kyrgyzstan - one of the 15 countries that declared independence when the USSR fragmented into so many pieces that if you walk this territory, your two feet may actually be in two different countries, one of which might (or might not) be Kyrgyzstan. Kyrgystan's (pronounced "wow!") claim to fame is that it's the only country in the world with just a single vowel in its name.

Multi-tasking - A euphemism that means an inborn or acquired talent to ruin as many tasks as possible simultaneously. A multi-tasker is someone who can talk on the phone while cooking, watching the baby, and working on the computer. Obviously this someone is a woman who has the ability to watch milk boil over very calmly as she--again very calmly--tries to prevent her baby from eating a knife while her PC quietly self-destructs in a corner and her significant other watches WWF in a semi-conscious state. A man's idea of multi-tasking is watching TV AND eating potato chips.

Peace of mind - a concept made scarce by man, peace of mind is now the hottest selling topic for wannabe writers. Peace of mind is something you have until the moment you pick up a book on it. There's no absolute peace of mind - it just depends on who's trying to define it where. In Iraq, Afghanistan, parts of Africa, Pakistan, and the "West Bank," peace of mind means not getting killed; in the rest of the world, it means not knowing who's getting killed where; in America, peace of mind means killing everyone everywhere while skipping around the world with a goofy smile, a twinkle in your eye, and bombastic rhetoric. In Italy, it's watching someone at the lunch table being garrotted with a piano wire while licking pasta off your fingers and crying with the opera soprano. In India, it's TV dinner at 9 p.m. with news channels outdoing each other to wake up the dead. In the Arctic, no one knows or cares what peace or mind is which of course is true peace of mind.

Rediffmail - an email service whose users belong to a large, happy, close-knit spamily where everyone is on first (and only) name basis. Rediffmail users can live their entire life within its inbox where they can shop, get a degree, go abroad, buy tickets, buy books, sell auto parts and body parts, buy movies, music, houses, insurance, hire, get hired, make friends, become a star, get married - all at bargain rates in limited offers.

Singapore - a squeaky clean city-state where long jump is banned in schools - the kids might fall into the sea or into Malaysia which just might trigger World War III. Singapore is apparently the most "business-friendly economy" in the world - it should be - Singapore's national passtime/national sport is shopping.

Stock market - one of modern day's greatest mysteries, the stock market can take entire economies to the cleaners simply because it rained in Timbuktu while semi-paralyzed men in drenched shirts, loosened ties, and with glazed eyes have fingernails for lunch and heart attacks for dinner trying to understand why the Dow Jones cannot behave as ordinary as it sounds.

Summer - Long ago, summer was one of 4 seasons - the other 3 being winter, monsoon, and spring. Over the years, they all merged and became one season called Famine. But people the world over, didn't want a season called Famine - which is a combination of 'fashion' and 'feminine.' A few wars later, Afghansistan which was the only country that wanted the season to be called 'Famine,' gave up its demand after incessant bombings caused the country's first floods that had a free run in the territory simply because there was nothing and no one left standing to stop it and it was agreed unanimously to call this season Summer. There are varying degrees of Summer:

    Mild Summer

    Please-wring-my-blouse-again Summer

    Have-you-caught-fire-yet? Summer and

    Do-not-disturb, I'm-in-coma Summer

United States of America - the friendly neighbourhood rogue elephant that won't get out of your backyard, the USA's chief hobby is to create, protect, and destroy its own creations. A largely bored, ADHD-suffering population with a collective attention span of 2 seconds, America loves democracy but can't spell it, wants all the world's oil but won't pay for it, and is burning up the ozone faster than it burned up Iraq but--like with Iraq--refuses to fix it. America also makes people rich and forgives them for some time for being rich because of it. The original master of hype, America is the only country in the world with its own tagline: "Coming soon to a theater near you!"

Venezuela - Cuba's oil-rich friend that supplies around 80,000 barrels of oil a day to Cuba which has helped make the U.S. embargo look like a long-running boring Hollywood flick that no one is watching. Venezuela has given the world many beauty queens and is a country where people keep chasing one another around the office block to become head of state. Venezuela's late President Hugo Chavez has grabbed countless hours of air time calling President Bush colourful names including "the devil" in a speech at the UN General Assembly which was met with "wild applause" in the Assembly and severe condemnation in the U.S.

"Falls alarms, do not picnic"

The shrieking fire alarm made me jump out of my skin. RRRRUUUNNNN, RRRRUUUNNNNN, RRRRRUUUUUNNNN, it screeched urgently. Around me, people stared intently at their computers, chewed gum, chatted, laughed – they were oblivious to the fire alarm. I've always been intrigued by this: if they were caught in an unexpected downpour, the same people who now sat through the fire alarm chewing gum, would run out of the rain like they were heading for a bomb shelter. We treat a silly shower like an air raid siren and a fire alarm like a coffee break bell! We'd rather be burnt toast than be wet! Had anyone ever heard of "priorities"!?! Did they expect the fire to walk up to their workstations, tap them on their shoulders and say "Hello! Shall we sizzle on the dance floor?"!?! Had everybody gone MAD!?! As I worked myself up into a righteous fury, a message flashed across our screens: "Falls alarms, do not picnic."

Then, a few seconds later: "FALSE ALARM, do not picnic."

Well, well…. and then: "Sorry, PANIC."

"Panic, people, panic!" I yelled and bolted like a bat out of hell screaming "Fire!! Fire!! Run!! Run!!"

It was only after I had clattered down a full flight of stairs at supersonic speed that I realized

a) No one else had picnicked…or panicked…or whatever.

b) There was no fire alarm blaring.

c) My left hand was attached to someone's right.

I turned and met a pair of icy eyes. "Whoa!" I yelped and staggered backwards, "Who are you?"

"My sentiments exactly," the owner of the hand replied frostily. "Thank you for saving my life. Now, if you don't mind…." she yanked her hand out of mine and turned on her heel and stomped out.

"You're welcome," I croaked.

I tried to slither back in unnoticed--I crouched and duck-walked but someone spotted me and called, "Welcome back!!" and I got a standing ovation. Where is that damn earthquake when I need it…!

MORAL OF STORY: 30 minutes a day 4 times a week, practise duck-walking.

The Tragedy of the Commons

In what is being dubbed as an unprecedented comic crisis, UN Secretary General departed from his textbook address to the UN to express his anguish at Archie's decision to marry Veronica. "Betty Cooper is all set to become a suicide bomber," he croaked in a strangulated whisper as heads of state looked on in horror. "No matter what we do, there's one born every minute," the distraught UN chief went on, looking and sounding dangerously close to a meltdown.

"It ain't over till it's over pal," an unidentified voice called from the back to nervous laughter.

The American President gamely tried to bring sanity to the situation by declaring, "It's recession time, folks. A loser like Archie is better off with the Lodges than out on the streets looking for work."

His comment was met with loud boos and desk thumping from one section and "hear, hear" from another.

"Always the bridesmaid, never the bride," was Britain's typically understated response.

"Excuse me! In my country, people are killing each other to eat mud!" exclaimed an enraged representative from the continent of Africa, "maybe you should fly your Archie and Veronica to my country for their honeymoon," he fumed in disgust.

The House descended into chaos with Russia, China, and Pakistan aggressively outbidding each other for discounted airline fares to the newlyweds.

When asked to comment, Cuba's leadership was blunt, "Archie can marry Veronica's mother for all we care."

"Or her father," was North Korea's laconic quip.

India has called for a 3-day closed-door meeting of the SAARC nations to decide what to decide. "We're monitoring the situation," was the only cryptic comment from the big brother of the subcontinent.

The Secretary General pounded the desk with his gavel for order causing the Israeli leader to jump up with a blood-curdling shriek as he looked at his shattered fingers in horror. The leader had to be straitjacketed and carried out to prevent him from firing a gun that he pulled on the shocked Secretary General.

"How did he get that in?" protested the Middle Eastern bloc. "This is a conspiracy. The infidel planned to assassinate us! All deals are off. We're blowing up Israel right now," they yelled and stormed out.

The Secretary General asked for a show of hands for Veronica and Betty assuring the House that he would force Archie to abide by the majority's wish. The USA, France, Italy, Australia, and China raised their hand for Veronica – and for Betty. Indian diplomats studied their feet and sat on their hands. An Iraqi diplomat hurled his shoe at the Secretary General but missed him and caught British Premier square in the face. "Bull's eye" muttered the French President unaware that he was caught on tape. England immediately severed all diplomatic ties with France.

"Please let us all calm down," pleaded the Secretary General. "In this hour of grave global crisis, it's important that we all stand together putting our petty differences aside."

"Yeah right," said a Bangladeshi diplomat, "after all, in my country only a few tens of thousands have been displaced by floods but clearly this is a far greater humanitarian crisis we have on our hands."

When asked to comment, the German Chancellor said, "I think I need a drink," and headed off to find one.

In May 2009, the creators of Archie comics announced that Archie will wed Veronica breaking millions of hearts around the globe and setting off furious debates about Archie's decision.

Vote for Tony Blair

My life is insured by a government owned insurance company, so I made my annual piligrimage recently to one of their anachronistic offices to pay my premium. Like government offices all over India, this one too was populated by groaning ceiling fans, irascible people with cobwebs, East India Company files, a forlorn-looking Gandhiji on the wall, and an unbalanced security guard in army fatigues and a whistle whom everyone called "Major". The walls, floor, and ceiling were all broken, stained, and leaking; each chair had a different missing part and I don't think there were any tables at all - files were piled so high in front of each person, no one would've noticed if Major had stolen all the tables and auctioned them to pay for his fatigues and his evening drink. Huge old steel cupboards were backed into far-flung corners and ominously locked with ponderous looking 18th century heavy metal. I was sure if someone unlocked them, decomposed bodies would tumble out ("Ok, we can now tell Mrs. Sharma to withdraw the 'missing persons' complaint she filed about her husband during the Quit India movement"). Glass panels separated the public from the mildly demented staff who sat behind the glass panel glowering, barking, and baring their fangs at the likes of me who tried to make them happy by paying them money for our lives - they were very bitter; being perpetually watched over by Gandhiji made their experiments with truth very uncomfortable.

I went to the section titled "PREMIUMS" and immediately noticed I was the only one there; there were serpentine queues at every other desk except this one; that was because the chair behind the glass panel was empty.

"AWOL," Major offered helpfully.

AWOL's colleagues turned and glared at Major and me and I quickly found an interesting pattern to study on the floor.

"Where should I pay?" I asked Major softly under my breath (for I didn't want to disturb grateful dead Gandhiji).

He waved his arm in a general north-east/north-west direction and yawned and I thanked God I was not lost in Kosovo with Major as my guide - then, I realized that actually, I was.

I joined the queue closest to me. Have you noticed inside a government office, people are scared to talk to each other? No one will help you (which on second thoughts might be a good thing because the blind leading the blind isn't such a good idea - look what happened to Tony Blair).

"Excuse me," I said softly to the person in front of me; he looked at me out of the corner of his eye but didn't turn around.

"Are you standing here to pay your premium?" I whispered.

He shook his head in a way that could mean, 'yes', 'no' or 'maybe.'

I looked around helplessly and decided to join a different queue.

"Excuse me," I whispered to the back of a new head.

"Shhhhh," he hissed without turning around.

Not knowing what to do, I approached the glass panel; the entire queue became restive and started to growl. I heard "queue," "line," "go back," and even "monkey".

"I just want some information," I said desperately to no one in particular.

"YES! WHAT DO YOU WANT?" someone barked from behind the glass.

"I want you to burst into flames," I almost said but of course didn't.

"Where do I pay my premium?" I asked timidly.

"WHAT DO YOU THINK EVERYONE IS DOING HERE STANDING IN THE QUEUE?" the voice spat back.

"I thought they're celebrating Kosovo's independence," I muttered and joined the queue. Someone giggled. "SILENCE PLEASE!" the voice thundered and everyone, amazingly, fell silent!

"Why shouldn't we talk? Has someone died?" I asked recklessly.

"MADAM, THIS IS AN OFFICE!!"

"Yes, I noticed it's not a funeral parlour," I said.

He muttered abuses under his breath (which I cannot repeat here due to lack of space).

When my turn came to pay, I paid up and asked for an ECS form.

"He's on leave," the non-combustible character snapped without looking up.

"Who? The form?" I asked.

"THE PERSON AT THE COUNTER WHO DISTRIBUTES THE FORMS IS ON LEAVE," he said slowly and loudly like talking to someone very vacant.

"Can someone else give me the form?" I asked.

"NO! COME TOMORROW!" he commanded.

"Yes, I'd love to see your pretty face again," I almost said but of course didn't.

The next day, they were out of forms; the day after was a public holiday; the day after that was a second Saturday; the day after the day after the day after the employees were on strike, and the day after all these days someone should've torched the place but didn't.

MORAL OF STORY: When you find him, vote for Tony Blair.

Insomniacs, Killjoys, and other friendly people

Even in my dream, I knew it was a dream. No cell phones. No sales people. No emails. I snuggled into my dream.

The telephone exploded. I fell out of bed and grabbed it.

"Hello," I croaked groggily.

"Good afternoon ma'am. I'm Raju from _____. As you're our valued customer, we're offering you a free SIM card..."

"Dear Raju from wherever you are..." I whispered half asleep and then fell into bed and right back into Dreamland. *Bengaluru had great roads. Everyone understood Mamata Banerjee when she spoke. Britney Spears had finally grown up. Newspapers ignored Paris Hilton and the Beckingham Palace. People admitted all they did in Davos was have fun...* the phone screamed again.

"Good afternoon ma'am. Are you Aparna Muralidhar?"

"Who wants to know?" I yawned.

"Ma'am, Aparna Muralidhar has won a trip for 2 to Malaysia in a raffle."

"What raffle?"

"Are you Aparna Muralidhar?"

"I am now."

"Congratulations Ma'am! You've won a trip to Malaysia!" he squealed.

"Okay okay, no need to get excited," I said irritably. "How did I win?"

"Are you married?"

"Not that I'm aware of..."

"You visited the exhibition at _____ with your husband where you filled in..."

"Shoot! I missed my own wedding," I muttered.

"...a form for a lucky dip on the 6th of this month at 10 a.m..." he prattled.

"I did not. I was at work."

"Are you sure?"

"Of course I'm not sure. I suffer from Alzheimer's. I'm never sure of anything. When can I go to Malaysia?"

"Err.. uh... ma'am are you Aparna Muralidhar?"

"I'm not sure," I said distractedly, "look what you've done... you've confused me," I said and hung up.

I curled up under the covers once more. *Reader's Digest was a great magazine again. Music was not recycled. Paper was. I was 18. Planes stayed in the air. Trains stayed on tracks. Buses crunched only gravel. Everyone had a last name. The phone was ringing....* THE PHONE WAS RINGING.

I groaned and snatched it from its cradle.

"Hello?"

"Good afternoon, ma'am. I'm Amit from _____ bank. We're offering you a personal loan..."

"Great!" I yelled into the phone. "I need a loan right now. I have Alzheimer's and I'm going to Malaysia with a husband I didn't know I had," I tried to sound as hysterical as possible.

"Hello!?!" he said perplexed.

"You can call Raju and check..." I yelled. Amit hung up.

I went back to bed.

I'd barely tucked myself in when the phone shrieked.

"Hello?"

"I'm calling from _____ insurance. We have a wonderful package..."

"Great! I'm going to Malaysia so I need travel insurance. Can you give me your number? I'll call you back."

He gave me his office number, his mobile number, and his home landline.

Bingo and big mistake.

I took the phone off the hook and slept till 12 a.m. I woke up at 12 a.m., dug out Mr. Insurance's home landline and dialled.

"Who is it?" demanded an alarmed voice.

"I just wanted to say I'm not going to Malaysia and I don't want insurance," I said sweetly and hung up.

For Mozart, press 5

"For customer service, press 1.
For your bank statement, press 2.
For your account balance, press 3.
For money transfer, press 4.
Or wait for operator's assistance"

I waited.

"Sasha, Customer Service Executive. May I help you?"

"Hello?" I said cautiously.

"Hello."

"Hello?" I said again.

"Hello!"

"Hello?" I said a third time.

"Yes! Hello! What can I do for you?"

I exhaled. Satisfied I was talking to a live human being, I said, "My name is Aparna Muralidhar…"

"Yes Sir?"

I winced. "I want "stop payment" issued…"

"One moment, Sir" she said and put me on Mozart.

I gritted my teeth and closed my eyes. A cheery image flashed across my mind's eye. I was skipping happily and singing "Joy to the World" in a brightly lit hall while I twisted Sasha's arm behind her back and held her head under water. I shook my head and the image passed. Mozart was interrupted.

"Raja, Customer Care Executive. May I help you?"

"Yes. My name is Aparna Muralidhar. I want stop payment…"

"Your account number Sir?"

"MISS!! M-I-S-S, MISS!!" I hissed.

"Sorry, there's no such number. Thank you for calling customer care. Have a good day Sir," he hung up.

I hung up calmly and dunked my head in the bucket of cold water that I always keep beside me when I call the bank. I wrapped a towel around my head, counted to 10, and dialled again.

"For customer service, press 1.
For your bank statement, press 2.
For your account balance, press 3.
For money transfer, press 4.
Or wait for operator's assistance"

I waited.

"Sasha, Customer Service Executive. May I help you?"

"Yes, I had called just now regarding stop payment…"

"One moment, Sir. I'll transfer your call…" Mozart.

"Raja, Customer Care Executive. May I help you?"

"Yes. My name is Aparna Muralidhar. My account number is…" I recited the 10-digit number. "I've issued a cheque that I want…"

"One moment Sir…yes, I have your account."

'Congratulations you twerp,' I thought. "As I was saying…"

"What is your birth date Sir?"

"8/5/1972 Madam" I sneered.

"And how old are you Sir?" He was apparently happy to belong to either gender.

"872 years Madam."

"One moment Mrs. Muralidhar...."

"MISS, MISS, MISS!!!! What are you? DEAF!?!?" I shrieked.

"Sorry Ms. Muralidhar. What can I do for you Sir?"

"I want to issue stop payment on a cheque," I said wearily.

"You'll have to speak to my colleague. I'll transfer the call, Sir..." Mozart.

"Keerti, Customer Relations Officer. Can I help you?"

"I hope so. Look, I've narrated this story thrice already. I just want a cheque to be stopped from being encashed..."

"Your account number Ma'am?"

I gave her the number.

"Cheque number, Ma'am?" At last we were getting somewhere.

"Sorry Ma'am, it's just been debited from your account a minute ago. Thank you for calling Customer Service Ma'am. Have a nice day."

You bet.

I counted to 10 and called the bank again. I was determined to have a nice day. When Sasha came on line, I said, "There's a bomb strapped to your chair, you twit. If you so much as breathe, they'll have to scrape you off the walls."

"One moment Sir," she said and put me on Mozart.

I Have a Dream

It was one of those days that hurtle from one Oh-my-God-disaster to the next and makes you want to crawl back into bed and sleep out the sunset. On my 287th oh-my-God, a voice boomed: "Yes? You called?"

I spun around. "I'm God. What's your problem?" the voice asked.

"You," I said unhesitatingly as I crouched and looked under my cot for God, "you're the problem."

"Get up... what did I do?" the voice asked.

"What did You do!?! The world is upside down in case You haven't noticed. Don't You see the mess? What DIDN'T You do!" I checked under the chair, behind the doors, under the bed cover...

"That's MY problem. What's YOUR problem?"

"Everything. I don't know what I'm doing with my life. I don't know what I want but it's definitely not this. I don't like this day. Nothing ever seems to go right. I feel homicidal."

"Okay. If I let you kill one person and get away with it, who would you want to kill that will help your days get better?"

I was shocked! "Only one!?!?" I said disbelieving.

"You're quite ambitious aren't you for someone who doesn't know what's going on?"

"If you're really God, I have some questions for you."

"Shoot."

"Do You answer everyone who says "Oh God!"? Why didn't You show up all these days? Did You really create George Bush? Why don't You stop people killing each other in Your name? Why do floods happen? And earthquakes, and tornadoes, and epidemics? Why do children die? Why was I born? What is the...."

"Whoa.. whoa... stop already!" the voice boomed, "so this is all MY fault now?"

"Well, You should at least own moral responsibility and resign!"

"And then what? You'll take my place?"

"Hmmm... now, there's an original thought!

"Just for the record... someone--I don't know who--created George Bush when I logged out for a bathroom break."

"Just what I needed--a God who's a joker."

"What's wrong with that?"

"Nothing really, but I hope you don't think this is funny?"

"Well, isn't it? By "this," I'm assuming you mean the state of the world – it's living proof that I have a sense of humour."

"We don't like your jokes, and by "we" I mean the rest of the world."

"Go to hell."

"My God! You're GOD!! How can You talk like that? Besides, I'm already there."

"You're very ungrateful..."

"Oh, c'mon," I waved my hand dismissively, "don't tell me you're going to lecture me about all the beauty you've created that we're destroying... about your rainbows, your forests, the Arctic, and the butterfly... it's hard enough to read it in my mailbox every day... there's even a mail where you talk to your "son" (like you're talking to me now)," I giggled, "you tell your son 'always remember I love you, and I'm always there for you,' or words to that effect." I giggled some more.

"And you find THAT funny?"

"Who's that guy who said 'If you talk to God, you're praying. If God talks to you, you're schizophrenic'?"

"A schizophrenic."

"I can't believe I'm having this conversation! How do I know You're God at all? You're probably some nutcase who's hiding very well somewhere and being a smart ass."

"Same thing."

"Ok, I'm not going to engage in this witless banter with a voice. Just give me a readymade solution that I can implement right here, right now."

"Chuck your job and get a life. Travel, meet people, write poetry, learn to sing, play the piano, paint... in short, take that mail seriously."

"Somebody, help!" I screamed, "Dunk me in cold water! This can't be real!"

Immediately, an avalanche of ice cold water hit me and knocked the wind out of me. I shot up in bed, drenched and speechless.

My 5- and 3-year-old nephews stood there holding an empty dipper and their sides, laughing like only kids can.

Laughter, the bitter medicine

Have you ever been attacked by hysteria at the most inopportune moment and dissolved into helpless peals of hideous laughter that made everyone who crossed your path stumble backwards with raised eyebrows, dropped jaws, and soundless screams? It happened to me just the other day.

I was in an auto on my way to work at 2 p.m. - a situation in which sane people would be at their waspish best which is how I am most of the time. I must confess I'm not given to easy laughter for many reasons: 1. My teeth don't exactly qualify for a toothpaste ad. 2. My nephew told me the first time that he heard and saw me laugh, that I sounded and looked like a "hyena" - it's not very original but if you hear it from a 2-year-old close to tears, it is. 3. Life IS funny anyway. Why laugh and compound your misery? 4. Imagine a startled cat wheezing laboriously while being spun around in a washing machine and you'll know what I sound like when I laugh.

Some long-forgotten memory popped into my sun-touched head and what started as a quiet chuckle, proceeded to a prolonged giggle, then grew into a throaty laugh (see point #4 above for definition of "throaty"), and then seemingly got away from my hands.. or is it my mouth?... or is it my belly? Where DO laughs originate anyway? (Don't answer)

As the rickety auto bounced along, I sat in the back seat struggling to get a hold of my contorted facial features. The auto driver at first was just annoyed, then distracted, then seriously worried, and finally downright terrified. "Should I stop?" he asked turning back, sending me into fresh bouts of hysteria. He turned around and continued to drive. For as long as I live, I will never forget the look on his face.

He picked up speed so that the unsuspecting passerby who just happened to glance into the speeding auto saw a rigidly upright terrified driver with a hysterically gasping passenger flailing wildly in the back seat. Every time I saw a face like that on the road, I got hysterical afresh. Finally, I forgot the original source of my hysteria and began pointing, slapping my thigh, and throwing back my head and roaring at anyone who dared to look into the auto.

The auto continued to hurtle along and in my state, I failed to notice that the driver had sped past my office, till he'd gotten away a good distance. When that realization dawned, my hysteria disappeared instantly and I barked at the auto driver to stop. He turned around and saw my bared fangs and heard my rumbling growl and promptly fainted. I left the money on his head, got out, and cussed loudly as I trekked to my office in the baking sun.

"… so tell us something about yourself…"

I'm sure it was just some sort of allergy because as I entered the office, I saw someone talking and laughing on the phone. I marched up to him and wordlessly socked his jaw. Then, I turned around and went home and slept. When I woke up at 10 p.m., mercifully, I was completely cured.

The Salesman

Good afternoon madam, myselfxxfromyy products this is a promotion just one minute open the door madam" - the apparition rapped outside my door.

"Huh?" I blinked as the afternoon sun blinded me and I tried to find my bearings. The doorbell had shattered my siesta and I'd sprung out of bed and landed at the front door, unaware that I'd moved. I tried to focus.

"Justoneminuteopenthedoormadam" he danced to an imaginary beat. I looked at him incredulously. He had a grinning mask on, which he had now pushed up on his forehead to give me the real all 32 whites. There were two macabre grins on his face. On his head, he wore something that looked like rabbit ears and flapped violently when he spoke. He was dressed in colours to help you spot him from outer space, and he had a yo-yo in one hand that squealed, a puppet that quacked in the other, and a huge bag on his shoulder that undoubtedly contained other such noisy nightmares that pass for toys today.

"What do you want?" I asked unable to keep the edge out of my voice. Try keeping your cool when you discover you've been woken up by a dancing monster rabbit from hell at 3 in the afternoon.

"Justoneminuteopenthedoormadaaam," he said again.

"What language are you talking?" I asked genuinely surprised. For a ludicrous moment, I wondered if he'd really landed from Mars.

"Harharharhar" it laughed and I reeled backwards. Surely, this was just a bad dream.

"Just one minute open the door madam," he said slowly with an ear-to-ear grin like he was addressing a 2-year-old retard. "I have wonderful imported toys, cheap madam, great fun for whole family, not just for childrens, nicetimepassopenthedoormadam."

"I don't want any toys!" I said unable to believe I was having a conversation with a Martian. "Don't buy madam, just see," he said, grin in place, and began to set his bag down.

"No!" I screamed in a panic. "I don't want to see any toys! Why would I want to see toys?"

"Buy for your children madam, see madam this talking parrot here; you put the battery here, wind it here and see madam, see, see.... it's imported madam" he danced and grinned.

I twisted my neck from 20 to 360 degrees to see from which angle it would look like a parrot and finally gave up. The contraption was talking in an unknown tongue at an ear-splitting decibel. I covered my ears instinctively and nodded my head violently to indicate to him that he should leave and take his foreign monster with him. He put away the parrot and took out a kangaroo.

"How about this madam? Jumps very nicely, just do like this, like this, like this, like this, like this, like this... er... uh... it's not working, Iwillshowyouothertoys oneminuteifyouopenthedoormadam" the grin never faded.

"There are no children in this house and I don't really play with toys, so please leave, and close the gate behind you," I said and turned to walk in.

"Just you open the door and see what other things I have madam. I have books also, just see, you don't have to buy" Didn't his face tire grinning like that?

"I really don't have the time and I must ask you to leave," I said trying hard not to abuse him.

"What about mobile phones madam? Do you want a cell phone?" Grin, grin.

"NO!" I said, exasperated.

"Life insurance?" Grin, dance.

"LIFE insur.. uh?" I couldn't make the switch.

"What about flats?" Grin, grin, dance dance.

"Do you have that in your bag as well?" my eyes were wide with astonishment.

"Or an electric oven? Or do you want car covers? Do you have a garden? (he was standing in my 2-foot space) Do you want an apple tree sapling? Money-back guarantee is there... mattresses? Sofa backs? Nightdress? Grin, grin, grin, dance, dance, dance.

I honestly couldn't understand what I was feeling at that point. I was being verbally assaulted by a wiry schizophrenic with two grins who was carrying the world and a zoo in his bag and wouldn't get off my property. I'd never felt more alone in my life.

I looked around wildly.

"Okay give me a glass of water then" he said suddenly and stepped closer to the door. I was sure I could detect a manic glint in his eye and I shuddered.

"If you don't give me a glass of water, you'll be born a lizard in your next birth. Do you want me to read your palm? I can predict the future. Just tell me the time you were born and I will tell you everything that is going to happen in your life. I can show you the lizard that you will look like in your next birth. It's right here in my bag," he began to dig into his humongous sack, never losing the grin.

"Can you really predict the future?" I croaked.

"Yes," he said in a steely voice and with the manic glint and of course the grin.

"Tell me how long you see yourself standing on my property then," I squeaked.

"I have Eric Clapton's and B.B. King's Riding with the King - you want? you can listen on iPod and decide if you want to buy - here, openthedoormadam and take this iPod -you can load 320 songs, listen while driving, eating, sleeping, reading, bathing, dressing, anywhere and everywhere," the energetic schizophrenic continued to rap and grin.

I felt lightheaded, nauseous, and close to hysteria.

"Givemeaglassofwatermadam, and I'll go," he danced, grinning.

"… so tell us something about yourself…"

"I'd rather be a lizard!" I growled, suddenly livid. "Get off my property or I'll set the dogs on you!" I screamed.

"Have a good day madam," he said, his ears flapping violently, both grins intact on his face, and turned to leave.

That's when I saw the huge tiger tail behind him.

10 things you must know if you're a road user in Bengaluru

#1. Zebra crossings are for zebras. People will cross 1 cm in front of whatever you're driving.

#2. Autorickshaws are 3 wheelers whose sole purpose of existence is to get in your way.

#3. All cyclists suffer from bipolar disorder. In their manic phase, they will chase buses. In their depressive phase, they will suddenly get off the cycle, carry it, and walk.

#4. When you see a bus in your rearview mirror, pray.

#5. When you see a pothole in front of you, honk - it might move.

#6. Do not swear. Share. You have as much right to the road as the holy cow.

#7. The light will always turn red when you're approaching it at 80 km/h.

#8. A truck's brake will only work after it has hit the object in front of it.

#9. Always tank up. The road you took to work in the morning will turn one-way by the time you return in the evening.

#10. Do not mess with traffic cops. They're from Mars.

The Psychometry

Lucky you! I flunked the Psychometry... again! Anyway, that's enough about me. If **you** want to take it up sometime in the future, I've designed this forerunner..... so, you're invited to take the Mock Psychometry to prepare you for the real thing.

It's in 3 parts: Analytical skills, Numerical skills, and English.

Part I - Analytical Skills

1. Peter is Jane's husband's brother's nephew's grandfather. Jill is Peter's wife's aunt's sister's step-mother (who is Jane, a.k.a. Cinderella's step-mom)
Question: a) Who is Peter to Jill?
b) More importantly, who are you to any of them?

2. Some mice are cats. All cats are donkeys. Therefore:
a) Cats are donkeys with Down's syndrome.
b) We have a strange menagerie here.
c) Mice are people too.

Think, you dunce.

Part II - Numerical Skills

1. A frog is in a 300-foot deep, 40-foot wide well and he's trying to get out. He jumps up 5 inches in an hour and slips back 1 foot. He started doing this in the 19th century. Question: How old will you be when the frog (or his fossil) gets out?

2. X bought a bike for Rs. 800 inclusive of 20% sales tax. He rode it for 45 days at 40 km per hour, 100 km a day. Calculate:
a) How much gas will he need to get himself to the moon on his bike?
b) How many days will he take? Convert to hours.
c) What percentage of his life will he spend doing this? Draw a graph.
d) How much money will he need? In paise and cents only.

Part III - English

1. Grammar:
a) I is fine.
b) What is the singular of mouses?
Question: Are this correct?

2. Punctuate correctly: How many legs do a cow have!!!

3. Subject-Verb Agreement:
Why is it wrong to say "I am dead tomorrow"?
a) Because I are still alive tomorrow.
b) Because I is dead yesterday itself.

c) Nothing's wrong - rest in peace.
d) Because I'm going to kill you NOW.

About the Test
The psychometry is designed to help determine whether you're good at managing people, your time, and yourself. It's not an IQ test (though the last time I flunked, the testing personnel came all the way to the office to tell me I have the creative intelligence of a retard ant). Go for it, you have nothing to lose except your ego, but that's nothing a good night's sleep (and a shot of cocaine) can't fix.

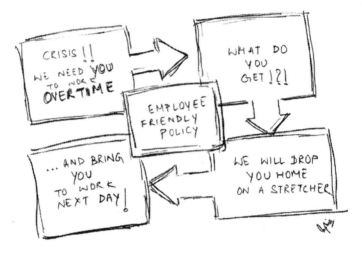

BREAKINGNEWS

This is to inform you that a revised and improved Overtime and Conveyance Policy has been posted on our Intranet. As you all know, we're in a perpetual crisis. Everyone knows this - you know, your parents know, your spouses know (or is it spice?!?... anyway...), your children know (if you have kids at home who're just learning to talk, the first word they'll utter will probably be 'crisis' - do not be alarmed). So, in order to encourage you to clock in extra hours, we revisited our OT and Con (short for conveyance - please don't get any ideas) Policy.

How you access this is: You log into the intranet, wait for 2 hours; click on HR Manual, wait for 2 hours; click on Policies, wait for 2 hours (please don't forget to work while you're doing all this waiting), click on Overtime and Conveyance Policy.... and come back tomorrow and read it. Because you can only read it tomorrow, the policy has been summed up here briefly.

Overtime Policy

Remains unchanged. You'll be paid the same rate per hour that you've always been paid. This is in keeping with our motto: "If you keep doing what you've always done, you'll keep getting what you've always got."

Conveyance Policy

For overtime upto 4 hours: Use your own conveyance and we'll reimburse you - at actuals or lesser (whichever is lesser.)

For OT upto 8 hours: OT vans will be provided (please bring your own driver).

For OT upto 16 hours: OT ambulances will be provided (please carry your medical insurance papers on your person.)

For OT greater than 16 hours: In-house IV drips and soft pleasant music will be provided.

Other Floor Luxuries

For overtime upto 4 hours: A good OT system will be provided. At the end of 4 hours, security will call a cab for you if you're without wheels. If you have wheels, valet services will be provided (please ensure that your vehicle is insured.)

For OT upto 8 hours: A good OT system and fresh orange juice will be provided. Security will escort you into your shuttle and strap you into your seat (new seat belts have been added in all vans.)

For OT upto 16 hours: A good OT system, fresh orange juice, and four 50-50 biscuits will be provided. Stretcher will be brought to your workstation and you'll be peeled from your chair and carried down on the stretcher into your OT ambulance. If you're embarrassed riding downstairs lying in the stretcher, you may sit up and crack jokes.

For OT greater than 16 hours: See under Conveyance Policy 'For OT greater than 16 hours.' In addition, one member of your family will be allowed on the floor to hold your hand and cry.

If any part of this is not clear, please write to us or come up and meet us and we'll fire you on the spot because, c'mon, if you can't understand something this simple, it's no wonder we're perpetually in a crisis…. let's roll, folks!

Who Are You?

I'm not what you would call gadget-savvy (give me a Remington typewriter any day). Here's why: I've logged in with my password, terminator (really, that's my password) for as long as I can remember (and here's my user ID: Harry. Go on, make my day). My computer usually welcomes me with this message: "Good Morning Harry Terminator. Have you told your neighbour about our referral scheme? If your neighbour joins us, we'll give you 30 paise extra every month for six months! Tell your neighbour now, Harry! TELL!" to which I would smile coyly and reply, "no, really, I can't take advantage of your generosity." And thus, life went on. Imagine my shock then, when one day I logged in as usual and my computer asked me "Who are you?" What a question! How am I supposed to know!?! Those of you who know the answer to the question "Who Are You?", raise your legs....... There! Some questions are best left unanswered.

Anyway, after much cajoling and coaxing and threatening, I discovered that my computer wanted me to change my password...... Oh! Did I tell you my password is 'terminator'? Sorry! I changed it. It's now 'exterminator' (and you can still make my day because my user ID is still 'Arnold'). I also discovered that, like everything else, my computer too was made in China, and that terrified the living daylights out of me. The Chinese (in competition with the Japs) make phones that can take your picture, double up as a computer, sing songs for you, send messages to your neighbour who's sitting less than half a foot away, play games, and in some cases, even shoot you if you press the wrong buttons long enough. You can also make calls (if you have the time). I have one such phone.... at home..... somewhere..... I'm saving money to buy a microscope to look for it. Anyway, that's why I'm not gadget-savvy. In fact, I'm petrified of anything that vaguely resembles buttons.

Addendum: The Japs will wait for the Chinese to come up with the inventions and then simply buy the company and patent the products and run around claiming it's theirs. (Unrelated to any of the above, an addendum literally means 'add' to the 'end'.....'ummm' - as in 'this is an after-thought').

Moral of Story: Learn Chinese. Your next Manager will be Made in China.

"There's a Bomb on the Bus....."

I was bored. I looked at the clock - "1 more hour to go!" it screamed. I twiddled my thumbs idly, and for some inexplicable reason thought of Keanu Reeves. His immortal line from Speed jumped at me out of the blue and suddenly I had - "a great idea!"

I sent a message on the chat to our front desk - "There's a bomb on the bus" - I sat on my hands and waited - 5 minutes passed, nothing happened; 10 minutes, still nothing; 15... nada; I crept down the stairs slowly and peeked at the front desk. The receptionist was on the phone. I hid from view and watched. She hung up and turned to her monitor. She frowned, she rubbed her eyes, she looked around, she frowned harder... then, she shrugged and went back to her work.

I charged - "Didn't you get my message!?!?" I asked incredulously.

"Oh... you sent that..?" she asked unruffled.

"Yes!" I almost screamed and waited expectantly... she continued working. "There's a bomb on the bus!!!!" I gesticulated wildly.

"What bus?" she asked looking up and leaning back in her chair.

"How should I know!?!?!?" my eyes were huge and incredulous with disbelief.

She shrugged again and gave me a 'where-did-you-escape-from?' look and went back to work.

"Aren't you going to do something!?!?!" my voice rose to a shrill pitch.

"What do you want me to do?" she asked without looking up.

"Well... how about looking up at me for a start!!!! Aren't you worried? People are going to die!!!"

"People die all the time..." she said. I couldn't dispute THAT.

"Do something!!!" I commanded.

"Well.... I can sing pretty well..." she offered sarcastically.

"Send everyone to the lunchroom!!!" I suggested ignoring her last remark.

"Why? Because there's a bomb on a bus somewhere in the city?" she asked

"What bus?!?!?" I yelled.

"How should I know?" she shot back… "You're the one that sent the message."

"Is that what I said!?!? No, no, I meant there's a bomb in this building!!!!" I was hysterical.

"Oh..?" she said.

'Oh' what!?!?!… evacuate everyone then… send a message and ask everyone to go to the lunchroom. NOW!!!" I barked.

"Go to the lunchroom" she said yawning

"Just me!?! What will I do there all by myself!?!? Tell EVERYONE!!"

"I can assure you no one will want to go to the lunchroom now" she said.

"Tell them what I told you!!" I was talking very loudly.

"That there's a bomb on the bus?" she asked.

"No, no, that there's a bomb in the lunchroom! Then, everybody WILL go!!!" I screamed.

She looked at her watch and got up. "Look, you'll miss your shuttle, and I'll miss mine… why don't you go home and take your tablets and get some sleep?" she was already on her way out.

"Oh... ah... yes..." I mumbled and followed her tamely.

As I passed the security officer's cabin, I saw him glued to the TV. I peered in - Maria Sharapova was on center court in her night clothes under the blazing Aussie sun.

"It's hot there, isn't it!" I remarked.

"You bet" the security officer grinned.

"Psst..." I said, gesturing for him to come closer. He leaned out.

"There's a bomb on center court" I whispered.

"I know" he said.... and winked.

The Humble Monkey Stands up to be Counted

"O, hear me all ye mortals, I have something important to say,
(Ignore this precarious coconut tree perch)
I just met Darwin the other day.
I said to him, 'Sir, I believe in Adaptive Radiation..'
To which, he drew himself up and replied rather impressively,
'Sir...' (yes, he called me that)
'Your posishun in the scheme of evolushun is a rung below mine,'
(He scratched his beard, perhaps for a simian touch)
'Besmirch not my reputashun, Mankind likes me fine.'
(When his brow knitted, I had to wonder whether we were separated by a rung at all)
'Hear me, dear ancestor,' I said, 'I've been here longer than you,
I've spoken to the dinosaur, I've spoken to the dodo, and to the cockroach too.'
(When he gnashed his teeth, I had to wonder whether our rungs had been exchanged.)
'No debate shall ensue, Sir,' he thundered
'My theory has survived religion

Sparring with you will consign to oblivion
All previous records establushed by our class
For descent from the sublime to the ridiculass.'
(When he snorted, I had to wonder whether your class had
descended from the bull)
'O, hear me all ye mortals, I have something important to say
I tried to tell Darwin I agreed with him but I happened to
lose my way
And when I lost myself, I found the Truth
And the Truth has set me free:
I challenge his theory of Variashun
(Men are all alike, you see)
I refute his allegations of Overproducshun
(My class is a dwindling populashun)
With his "Struggle for Existence" theory, I totally agree
But I still have a problem with the "Survival of the Fittest"
(The extinct dinosaur has put that to the test)
O, hear me all ye mortals
No race has survived so well like your own
(But certainly, your class is not the fittest in town)
Prophets proclaim "the meek shall inherit the earth one day"
In Darwin's absence, please allow me my say:
(Darwin is busy, now Mars needs a theory of evolushun)
All things considered, man is as timid as a mouse
(Except, of course, maybe in his own house)
So, the meek have already inherited the earth
(In our Animal Kingdom, your class is the object of much
mirth)
And, Eureka! Religion did win after all
Despite Darwin's claims so tall."

"… so tell us something about yourself…"

A Wedding and Other Hair-Raising Events in God's Own Country

I'm sure you've seen the Samsung ad with its large-hearted tagline "Everyone's Invited". That, in a gist, is a Kerala wedding - everyone's invited - and unlike in the ad, they'll all show up. The last time I attended a wedding in Kerala was 16 years ago when, if nothing else, age was on my side. 16 years later, on the wrong side of Life, the lethal combination of rain, heat, noise, and crowds to rival the best attended soccer matches prove a little too much for my feeble heart. It puts me in a perpetual state of near syncope for the entire duration of my stay.

There is one thing, however, to be said for weddings in the temple town of Guruvayoor (where my cousin took the plunge). Even if you're permanently lost, like I was, you'll get to attend SOME wedding - like I did - because there are so many happening on the day one of your own decides to seal his fate. I lost the crowd I was with (my mother's family that is roughly the size of two cricket teams with extras) which is very easy to do and ended up gazing at the bridegroom wondering if my handsome cousin's face could be so rearranged within 24 hours.

"Baaaangloooor allllaaayy??" someone screeched while grabbing my hand and I spun around to face an all-32 grin that belonged to the owner of the eardrum-shattering voice. I laughed inspite of myself. In Kerala, everyone (specially people you meet for the first time in your life) will squeeze your hand, pat your cheek, and stroke your hair and if you're the touch-me-not sort, the experience can be quite.... well, touching. Her smile was infectious and I happily let her take my hand and lead me back to where, she thought, I belonged - the mob that I'd been trying to lose ever since landing. On the way, she reeled off everything she knew about me (which was no surprise because by now I knew that people you've never seen before and probably will never see again know more about you than yourself) - from my vital statistics down to what I had had for breakfast that morning. Some of her facts were naturally completely divorced from reality, but who cares - I was having a ball!

The one thing that you absolutely do not want to be in a Kerala wedding is a single over-the-hill woman. You're a sitting duck (or a moving target - take your pick) for every whacko jacko and his mom, especially his mom, who has come to take a peek at you because her daughter's brother-in-law's aunt's husband's second cousin told her to....... but she's very suspicious that you're not married at such a ripe old age. She also thinks all Bangalore girls are "fast." She wants to know if you're: A. Mentally challenged. B. Physically challenged. C. Cannot have children. D. Recently ditched. E. All of the above. F. If others, please specify. You want to tell her where she should go with a one-way ticket that you'd be happy to buy for her, but she can't understand your language and you can understand hers perfectly.

Temples or temple weddings, however, are not the most divine experiences in God's Own Country - being a passenger in any mode of transport is. It's divine because you'll pray to every God you know as you shut your eyes tightly and nearly kill yourself holding your breath as you're dragged through the streets at breakneck speeds, dodging death by hair breadths. Every male driver on the road (this includes all the males in my family too) is a maniac. The morning of the wedding, I opened the paper and caught the news that 5 employees of the Indian Oil Refinery were smashed to smithereens in their car that collided head on with a bus. There was a photo of the car - it looked like a dismantled jigsaw puzzle that you could pack into your overnight bag and carry effortlessly. With this vivid picture and all the gory details of how the occupants were scraped free fresh in my head, I board Cinimol (isn't that cute !) In Kerala, buses have names, not numbers. Cinimol is a benign looking bus...... till it starts moving. On the back of the bus is emblazoned "CONCORD" in a fiery red which the fiend behind the wheel seriously believes. As he hurtles down the road at breakneck speed, he defies every law, every rule, every force of nature and gravity known to man. I pray incessantly and I thank God I'm in the bus and not out of it..... on the road..... in his way; if that happens, I'll only have enough time to hope that God doesn't run buses in Paradise.

When I alight, my internal organs are dancing to their own tunes as they try to find their spot to settle down. Cinimol races with Ranjinee's (not my punctuation or spelling) who's in turn racing with Highness and they're all trying to catch up with Sleeba (I couldn't make this up if I wanted to). I marvel that there are no bodies piled up on the streets. I promise myself never to ever again curse Bangalore drivers who're such lambs in comparison.

"Road Clossed" (not my spelling) the sign says. It's a challenge too inviting to pass up for my auto driver. At first I think he doesn't know English (or he knows better English), so I ask him "closed alllaayyy??" He looks at me and laughs and says it's been closed since 1947 and he's been using it for roughly the same period. I want to scream, "but where is the road?" but I underestimate this champion driver. He's already delivered me to my destination in one piece - as usual, I wasn't looking. I feel like falling on my knees and thanking him.

When it's time to leave, I don't want to go. This is a pace of life that is forgotten in my world (if you forget the traffic part). People have time for you here. They're interested in what you say. They're simple, they're great hosts, and there are some parts of their human spirit that are still unspoiled by my world - just like their beautiful land. Most of all, they're open - what you see is what you get. I want to stay, but I can't..... of course, I'll always go back..... to my second home.